Andrew McDeere

SEED

SAVING

A Complete Gardener's Guide

to Learn how to Storage and Save Seeds of Vegetables,

Plants, Flowers, Fruits and Herbs

Copyright © 2020 publishing.

All rights reserved.

Author: Andrew McDeere

No part of this publication may be reproduced, distributed or transmitted in any form or by any means, including photocopying recording or other electronic or mechanical methods or by any information storage and retrieval system without the prior written permission of the publisher, except in the case of brief quotation embodies in critical reviews and certain other non-commercial uses permitted by copyright law.

Table of Contents

What is a Seed? 5

Saving Seeds 15

Why Save The Seeds? 22

Seed Saving - How to Save Money in an Organic Garden . 37

How to Save Your Garden Seeds 50

How Do Annual, Biennial, and Perennial Plants Differ? 55

Seed Saving Technical 62

Selection Of Seed Parents 68

Saving Seeds from Your Garden 76

Saving Seeds From Your Herb Garden 82

Save Seeds - How to Preserve Seeds for Tomatoes 85

Seed Harvest 91

Seed Extraction and Drying 95

Storage of Seeds 100

Dried Seed Collection 109

What is a Seed?

As a gardener, you probably managed hundreds or even thousands of seeds. But in order to become a successful seed saver, it is useful to learn what is inside these seeds and how plants form them in the first place. Although they are very small, the seeds are complex structures with an extraordinary capacity for growth and transformation. Essentially, a seed has three parts:

Embryo. The nascent plant, the embryo is the structure that will form roots and shoots as the seed germinates.

Endosperm. This integrated food feed feeds the embryo as it grows.

Seed coat. The outer shell of the seed protects the embryo. Although the seed is a hard shell, water and air can pass through it.

How Seeds Are Formed

Most garden plants are flowering plants and, as you know, flowers are the precursors of seeds. Flowers contain female (pistil) and male (stamen) reproductive structures. Some plants carry flowers that contain both male and female parts (they are called "perfect" flowers), and others carry flowers that contain only male parts or only female parts.

Pistilli. These can be large or small, and a single flower can contain one or more. A pistil consists of an ovary at the base, a tubular structure called Style, and a surface at the top of the style called stigma. There are eggs (immature seeds) inside the ovary.

Stami. A stamen usually has two parts: the anther and the filament. Anther is a bag-shaped structure that produces pollen. The filament is a thin rod, and the anther is located above it.

Pollination. Pollination is the transport of pollen from a plant to a pistil. Pollen can not move on its own, but many forces in nature can and make pollen move: wind, insects, water and even birds and bats. In home gardens, wind and insects are the two most important pollen factors.

Fertilization. A fascinating process occurs when pollen grains land on a stigma. Each pollen grain has two nuclei. A core feeds the formation of a tube that extends through the style to the ovary. The other core splits to form two spermatozoa, which travel along the pollen tube.

Eggs also have several nuclei. A sperm meets two polar nuclei, and this is the genesis of egg white. The other sperm merges with the nucleus of the egg to form what will become the embryo. This is fertilization - the beginning of seed development.

Parts of a seed

As difficult as it may be, imagine all the essential rudiments of a plant-leaves, stem and root- encapsulated in a small uniform bundle of life. This is really what each seed contains. Take the seed of an instant Bean, for example. Soak the seeds in water for a few hours, and slide the outer wall of the seed. It is easier to see, in the large seed of the bean, what is true for all seeds. There, compressed inside this hard outer coating, are a set of rudimentary leaves called cotyledons, a bud that looks like a small tuft of leaves, a stem from which cotyledons and shoots appear, and-at the opposite end of the stem—a tip of the root.

Each seed has inside a reserve of carbohydrates, fats, proteins and minerals to feed the dormant encapsulated plant. Some seeds, such as instant beans, Linden, watermelon and pumpkin, have thick, fleshy cotyledons (first leaves), which retain their food. In other types of seeds, the food supply of the young plant is found, not in the leaves, but in the endosperm, a material that occupies the remaining space in the integument, next to and around the plant, the embryo. The endosperm is floury in some types of plants; in others it is oily, waxy or hard. Buckwheat and most cereal seeds, for example, contain a floury endosperm.

A seed and its many parts

A smaller group, called monocotyledons, produces seeds containing a single cotyledon. As you may have noticed, the large family of herbs, to which corn, rye and other cereals belong, sends a single shoot when the seed germinates, rather than the paired leaves that form on most other vegetable crops. Onions, also belong to this group.

While some seeds germinate at any time, there are many others that follow an internal clock, a rhythm that ensures (as much as possible) that when the seed germinates, the conditions will be good for its growth. Some seeds must undergo cold or frosty temperatures to break dormancy. Still others need light to germinate. Lettuce seeds can refuse to germinate in the warm season, when the chances of success of the plant are lower than in the cool seasons.

If you only remember one fact from this eventful course in Botany, let it be this: the seeds are alive.

How the Seeds Are Formed

More than half of the plants that grow on our earth are flowering plants. Many flowers are small and unobtrusive, such as those of wheat and corn, but the seeds they produce have made possible some of the most influential plant improvements that people have been able to process.

The purpose of a flower in life is to produce seeds. Although the flowers differ enormously in color, size and complexity, each is specially equipped to form seeds.

Two parts of the flower are essential for seed production: the stamen, or pollen-bearing part of the plant, and the pistil, which receives pollen and feeds the future seeds. The long and thin stem of the stamen is called a filament. Pollen pockets at the ends of the filaments are anthers.

The stamen, with its filaments and the other, is sometimes called the "male" of the plant. The pistil, or "female" part, includes the stigma, or pollen-receptive region, the style, a long thin tube leading from the stigma to the ovary and the ovary itself, a cavity containing one or more eggs (eggs).

The parts of a seed

The seed is formed by the Union of a mature egg and a grain of pollen fertilizer. When a grain of pollen lands on the stigma of a receptive species, perhaps carried there by the wind or by a bee, it begins to grow, proposing a long thread of living matter that develops through the style, enters the ovary and enters an egg, where it enters the embryonic sac. The two cells - that of pollen and the "egg" - come together to form a single living cell, called zygote, which has the power to multiply. This unicellular zygote-very divided and enlarged and finally matured-becomes the embryo of the new plant, that rudimentary leaf-bud-stem root that is somehow all there even in the smallest of the seeds. The outside of the egg grows into the integument.

And what about the endosperm, this layer of food for the new plant? How is it formed? It is also an answer to this question; at least, botanists know what the process involves. (Why the complex impulses that cause these things to happen remains a mystery.) Although the pollen grain, at the first formation, was a single cell, it usually divides to form two cells by the time it reaches the stigma. One of these cells, you remember, joins the embryonic bag of the egg to form the zygote, which will become the embryo of a plant. The second cell joins other small parts of the embryonic sac - called nuclei-to form the endosperm, after much division and redivision of the cells.

The ovary, usually containing more seeds, grows in fruits, which are sometimes called vegetables, and which is often the final product of our gardening efforts. Examples are tomatoes and peppers.

Once the plant embryo inside the seed is fully formed, growth stops and the seed enters a dormant period during which, as mentioned above, the plant consumes small amounts of energy from the stored endosperm, just enough to keep it waiting."The seed is alive, barely, but it should not grow or develop until it is planted.

Saving Seeds

Poor weather conditions in the last growing season had a direct effect on seed availability this year. With such wet and rainy last year, downy mildew struck quickly and severely, spreading into the thickness of the oil. In addition to mold, wet weather nourishes other fungal diseases that can sweep your garden. In addition, the pure amount of water absorbed by the soil during a very rainy growing season can generate or even drown plants.

Many experts suggest buying seeds soon, as some types will soon be in great demand due to the small number of viable seeds available. And although often in America we can buy seeds from Europe, their season was as bad as ours, so this year we will not have the opportunity to buy from our neighbors in front of the lake. Some examples of seed producers will have difficulty finding this year are cucumbers, onions, carrots and sugar snap peas.

But all this by mixing, trying to find good and healthy seeds, it would not be necessary if all (or at least most) gardeners used to save their seeds. Seeds, provided they are properly stored, can be stored for years! So, if we have a bad growing season - or even two or three in a row - the wake seed would be nice, because they have a lot of seeds saved to use the next growing season.

Of course, the seeds you hold must be of the open pollinated variety. Hybrid seeds will not give a good harvest the second year, if anything, which means that you will be stuck in the endless cycle of having to buy and plant new seeds every year, regardless of the growing season of the previous year. By planting and saving pollinated seeds outdoors, you will be guaranteed to have vital seeds that will grow and produce healthy food for you and your family.

Also, since these seeds you saved come from a plant that grew in your garden the previous year, the seeds are already ahead of the game, in the sense that they are more suitable for your garden environment. Being forced to buy seeds from other parts of the country, or even from Europe, is a risky practice because you don't really know how these seeds will grow in your garden.

And finally, consider the money. Most of us are a little more "attached to money" now than we were a few years ago, and any opportunity to save money is an opportunity we should welcome. By saving our seeds, we save an average of $ 2.00 per seed pack. I know it doesn't sound like much, but your average gardener can buy a dozen different varieties of seed packs in a year, $ 24.00 of seeds. I don't know about you, but I can think of a lot of things I'd rather spend $24.00 on than seeds, especially when I know I can save seeds for free.

More gardeners have to start saving their seeds, exchanging their seeds and relying more on themselves and their immediate vicinity, than relying on the willingness to buy seeds from afar. As last season shows, if you wait or do not save your seeds, you will find yourself paying more for the varieties you want, if you can find them at the purchase.

Usually, during the winter months, our thoughts often turn to better weather themes like our proposed garden that we plan to start in the spring. We have already received seed catalogs from some of the leading companies showing their tempting seed selection for this coming season.

One of the usual comments you hear every year about this period is that there are not enough vegetable seeds for sale to compensate for demand due to the worsening food shortage situation. Although I do not think that this idea contains serious controversy, it reminds us of the fact that it would be better to use renewable garden sunflower seeds. With these seeds, we offer you the possibility of saving our seeds from one culture to another.

Even people who eat only organic raw foods will find that the seeds of these foods can be effectively saved for replanting if they wish. I had already written about saving the seeds of the simplest beginner plants such as beans, peas, lettuce, pepper and tomatoes and now I covered intermediate vegetables such as corn, various cucumbers, radishes, spinach and members of the pumpkin family, including pumpkin.

When considering the economy of corn seeds, it should be remembered that corn will suffer from depression due to inbreeding. If you use the same seed alone several plants, the resulting plants will show prickly growth, late maturity and less yield. To combat this problem, you should consider planting 200 corn seedlings and collecting seeds of at least 100 of the best you have.

Corn seeds can usually be harvested about six weeks after the con has reached its feeding stage which should be immediately after the shells have browned. Simply remove the skins and let the drying process finish.

Cucumbers also tend to depressive inbreeding, even if it is not as severe as corn. However, seeds should be collected from at least six cucumbers on six different plants. Keep in mind that the cucumbers you raise for the seed usually can not be eaten. They are left on the vine to ripen for at least five weeks at the end of their feeding phase. They should appear a golden color when they are ready to collect seeds.

During processing, slice the fruit, and then scrape the seeds with a spoon. Allow the seeds to stand more jelly liquid at room temperature in a jar for about four days. A fungus will form on top, so it is enough to stir or kiss every day. Gelatin will eventually dissolve, letting the seeds sink to the bottom. Spread the seeds on a few paper towels and dry them.

Unlike the above plants, depressive inbreeding is not a problem with Muskrat. Seeds can be harvested from ripe musky melon. Just wash the seeds clean rather than dry them on a towel.

With radishes collect the three-inch stems that contain the seed pods when the pods Brown and appear dried. Pull the whole plant and hang it in the same place to finish the drying process. Open the pods by hand to remove the seeds.

To store spinach seeds, wait for the plants to take Rosin, then remove the whole plant and hang it so that it dries. In an upward motion peel the seeds and put them in a container.

Make sure that when collecting pumpkin seeds that the plants are completely mature. This is usually indicated by a hardening of the outer shell. Let the plant heal for another four weeks after harvesting. Cut the hard shell open and collect the seeds. Rinse and dry with a towel. You have there now, you can prepare for next season.

Why Save The Seeds?

Numerous individuals save seeds for various reasons. Some do as such to protect an association with the past, developing an assortment that their parents have developed or cleaned where they live. Some do this to guarantee that the seed gracefully of an assortment is not, at this point accessible. Some have intentionally stood firm against current patterns in the neighborhood segment. A few, for example, the Seeds in the Heritage Seed Library, do as such to make surplus seeds that can be given to others. A few people save seeds since they generally do.

Hereditary disintegration

Maybe the most earnest motivation to save the seeds from a wide scope of plant assortments is to keep them alive and being used. Seed banks and reproducer assortments protect decent variety, however right now they are not open to the overall population who need to develop these assortments. While seed inventories offer as good as ever assortments every year, actually the decision keeps on contracting, as does the hereditary pool from which they are reared.

The primary purposes behind this loss of decent variety are a blend of lawful and business pressures. Notwithstanding, the consequence of hereditary disintegration is lost decision for the producer and an expansion in hereditary consistency in the fields.

Peril

There are a few issues brought about by hereditary disintegration.

Food security

With consistency, both hereditarily and as monoculture, comes the expanded danger of a parasite or malady that crushes a whole plantation. With consistency can come constraint in the cushion of an assault. Numerous assortments are as of now being utilized for our private food gracefully of the scope of hereditary data to empower them to adjust to new and evolving conditions.

Condition

Present day assortments have been reared to endure and require high dosages of substance pesticides and composts. These can endure in the earth, and many can possibly make harm people and other living beings.

Decision

For some cultivators, the primary explanations behind developing specific assortments are simplicity of gathering and capacity to travel, rather than taste. The flavor of the month is directed by what is proposed and what is and is continually advancing. What occurs if your decision isn't in the best ten makers or sowers?

Worldwide change

The homogeneity of assortments likewise doesn't consider the impact of environmental change. Nearby assortments were progressively regular since they developed well in territories where they were reared.

With environmental change, vermin, ailments, and agricultural practices (the requirements of natural cultivating are altogether different), a shifted determination will be fundamental. At the point when an assortment vanishes, the equivalent goes for conceivably helpful highlights, which we may not yet know, and once they are gone, they are probably not going to be recouped.

Arrangement

At present, the seeds are put away in long haul hereditary banks. This successfully freezes hereditary data inside them, giving a benchmark to what's to come. In any case, they are become just occasionally, regularly quite a while later, so as to refresh the stock, with the goal that a few highlights may not be known or taken note. As of now, these seeds will in general be accessible just for plant breeders, plant breeders, and researchers, yet not for the overall population.

Novices can keep their seeds, as has been accomplished for thousands of years, some time before the appearance of huge seed ranches and current farming. Along these lines, plant specialists are in charge of their own food. Enrolling your seeds each year permits your assortments to adjust to your condition. You will likewise have the option to see all the fascinating or valuable highlights, for example, protection from irritations or maladies.

There are numerous approaches to convey this seed, either through seed frameworks, for example, the Seed Heritage Library, or seed trade gatherings, a large number of which would now be able to be found on the Internet. Sparing seeds and developing your own food bodes well for an economical future.

FUNDAMENTAL BOTANY FOR SEED SAVERS

Classification

Every single living thing are characterized in a various leveled framework the advancement of which was begun in 1727 by Swedish researcher Carl Linnaeus. Linnaeus utilized two names for each sort of living thing. The principal name is the class; plants that are exceptionally similar to each other, for instance the sprinter bean and the French bean, share similar family, Phaseolus. The subsequent name is the species; sprinter beans are Phaseolus coccineus, while French beans are Phaseolus vulgaris. Since everything has two names, the Linnean naming technique is known as the binomial framework.

There are other frameworks of classification, above and beneath genera and species. Genera that share comparable attributes can be assembled into families, which thus can be gathered into requests and then classes. Classes might be gathered into divisions (or phyla). The entire domain of classification resembles the diagram of an incredible tree, with a couple of extraordinary appendages (orders); more branches, and a huge number of twigs (species).

Underneath species level might be one more gathering. So beetroot and chard are both Beta vulgaris, however beetroot is Beta vulgaris var. conditiva, while chard is Beta vulgaris var. vulgaris. Lower despite everything are developed assortments or cultivars. Hence there is a beetroot cultivar called 'Green Top Bunching' (complete name: Beta vulgaris var. conditiva 'Green Top Bunching') and another called 'Detroit' (complete name: Beta vulgaris var. conditiva 'Detroit').

The level at which seed savers are concerned is the conservation of the fundamental characteristics that recognize one assortment from another.

Blossoms

So as to make seeds, a plant must mate. This procedure includes blossoms, which convey the male and female conceptive organs. Frequently the male and female parts are contained inside a solitary bloom. This is known as the ideal blossom. Now and then, male and female parts are in discrete blossoms. These are blemished blossoms and might be framed on a solitary plant in which case they are named monoecious (Greek: mono, one; oikos, family unit), or they might be continued separate male and female plants. These are called dioecious (two family units).

Peas have 'great' blossoms

- Squashes are monoecious, with male and female blooms on a solitary plant.

- Spinach is dioecious, with independent male and female plants.

- Peas are great, with male and female parts in a solitary bloom.

The male piece of the bloom is known as the stamen, and the quantity of stamens is trademark to each plant species. Every stamen comprises of a fiber, at the tip of which is the anther. It is the anther that delivers the dust grains.

Male squash bloom, petals expelled

The female piece of the bloom is known as the pistil, which is separated into the shame, the style, and the ovary. The ovary contains at least one ovules, or egg cells. The shame is the piece of the pistil that is responsive to dust grains. It might be a clingy, handle like structure toward the finish of the style, or it might be a long bit of the style, as in the smooth tufts of corn.

At the point when a rich dust grain lands on an open shame, the dust grain shapes a cylinder that becomes through the style until it arrives at the ovary, where treats one of the ovules. In the long run, the ovary shapes the organic product or seed unit, while the prepared ovules form into seeds.

Fertilization

For seed to create, dust must be moved from the anthers to the disgrace. There are special cases, called parthenocarpic plants (Greek: parthenos, virgin; karpos, organic product) however they don't concern us here.

Dust and ovules convey the hereditary messages from the male and female plants separately. Sexual generation rearranges those messages, delivering posterity that contain a blend of attributes from mother and father. In the event that dust and ovules are from various assortments, the resultant seed will be a blend of those two assortments, rather than a trademark individual from a specific assortment (for example not consistent with type).

Seed savers must guarantee that an assortment stays unadulterated by confining the wellspring of the dust to a similar assortment as the ovule.

Some ideal blossoms prepare themselves. The anther may clear past the shame, as they do in the nasturtium, or the disgrace may develop past the anthers, as in the tomato. In some cases preparation happens before the bloom opens, as in the pea; this is called cleistogamy (truly, shut marriage).

For seed savers, self-preparation may make life simple, as in peas and most tomatoes, however these can likewise be cross-pollinated in specific conditions. At long last, a blossom might act naturally contradictory; it isn't fit for pollinating itself and must be cross-pollinated.

Cross-fertilization for the most part expects something to move dust starting with one bloom's anthers then onto the next blossom's shame. That something might be wind, water, or a bug or creature.

- Wind is the most troublesome specialist to control. Dust is exceptionally fine and can be conveyed significant distances.

- Water isn't significant for pollinating residential harvests.

- Pollinating creepy crawlies, for example, honey bees, are simpler to oversee. Frequently they can be avoided blossoms with a basic pen or sack. In other cases the seed saver may need to present substitutes for the common pollinators. See the Seed Saving Guideline

Seed Saving - How to Save Money in an Organic Garden

How can we ensure that all the seeds we sow in our organic gardens germinate and give us the plants? Wise gardeners store their seeds, year after year, especially seeds of rare inheritance. Of course, saving seeds also saves money. But the old seed often disappoints.

In case of doubt about the old seed, it is always wise to pre-germinate a test sample. Soak ten seeds overnight and lay them on damp kitchen paper in a warm place in a plastic bag. After a few days, this percentage shows signs of life. To do this, scientifically, you need to use at least 100 seeds. But it could be your whole hideout! Ten is a very good indicative title.

Do not lose the germination of seeds, of course. Pour it into a weak compost pot, with its barely visible growth tip, and water-ideally-with a diluted algae solution. Kelp is a great help for young plants.

If only 20% of your soaked seeds show life, you will know that - if you plant five seeds of your remaining stock in each form - there is a good chance that at least one seed will germinate.

If nothing germinates from the seed test, the seed is clearly dead or unnecessarily dormant. Eat the remaining seed! For example, in muesli or as a seasoning for homemade bread, depending on the type of seeds. Of course, not all vegetable seeds are pleasant to taste or eat and, of course, you would avoid commercially pretreated seeds. As the late John Seymour of the fame of self-sufficiency tirelessly puts it: "use that good old mother, common sense! "

The vitality of the seed is the real proof

About 75oF is the ideal germination temperature for almost all edible temperate plants. Eggplants, peppers, tomatoes, pumpkins and other plants in a warm climate prefer 85of them. But they still germinate pretty well at 75oF. Either way, we will know in about eight days if this batch of seeds will give us an example. 75% germination or only 15% germination. Or none.

Thus, when sowing in bulk, we can adjust the quantities of seeds accordingly, as we have seen. These tips will save you a lot of time lost, but... it is limited.

Why is that? Under ideal germination conditions, we could obtain, for example, the germination of 50% of parsnip seeds that have been very well preserved but are several years old. The manuals say that it is not possible to germinate the seed of parsnips, lovage, Angelica and other umbel lamps if it is much more than a year old and has been stored at room temperature.

(That said, the seed is full of surprises. One year I grew a large plot of parsnips, and many other umbel lamps too, from seeds that was verifiable five years and had been kept in my sock drawer.)

Why germination of internal seeds can give misleading results

If you germinate the seed of umbel lamps and many other plant species inside, the results can be misleading. Because parsnips do not take the transplant gently. They must be planted in situ, outside. So how can we test their likely outdoor performance without wasting a lot of seeds?

Answer: test the germination of these seeds under non-optimal conditions. The guy they will really meet outdoors. Spread your seed on wet kitchen paper, but place it for eight days in a cool, dark place with sharply fluctuating temperatures, for example, just above the freezing point at 28 ° C., or to represent the actual conditions in your garden.

For example, your garage in the spring? All the seedlings that emerge will give you a hint for the true percentage of vitality of this seed! Now you can sow the seed balance outside with confidence. (Or not.)

Grow your new variety of plants!

Here is another advantage of testing the seed in difficult conditions. If you pre-germinate the seeds in these conditions and plant only the surviving seedlings, you will really get very hardy plants. When they grow, save the seed from them. Provided they are pollinated outside (for example, not F1 or other hybrids), and you keep them from year to year and grow, you can grow and stabilize your unique variety. The one that is acclimated only for your Microclimate.

Seed Saving to Preserve Todays Bounty for Tomorrow's Gardens

Seed saving has long been the main way to transmit plants from generation to generation. Saving seeds is not only fun, but it is also an important way to perpetuate legacy plants and ensure the genetic diversity of the world's food crops, which are eroding at an unprecedented rate and accelerating. Seed saving has been successfully used for many crops over the years-the varieties we call "legacy" are here today because dedicated gardeners like you and I have faithfully saved the seeds over the generations.

Seeds are usually stored by annual and biennial plants. The seeds you save from your home production system are used for your climate and growth environment and are suitable for pests in your area. Seeds of hybrid varieties produce a mixture of offspring, many of which may have different characteristics from the parent. Seedsaving is easy; people have done it for thousands of years, in the process of breeding all the wonderful vegetables we eat today.

Saving the seed requires growing mature plants, and as a result, they become larger and stay longer than normal, so leave a little more space around them. Saving and cultivating seeds, year after year, participates in evolution. Saving seeds from heritage plants or native plants in your area is one way to maintain diversity in the area. Saving garden seeds at the end of each growing season can be a great saving measure and a way to duplicate last year's delicious harvest.

Plants are pollinated in three different ways, by wind, insects or what is called self-pollination. Plants of the same species can cross each other producing mixtures of the mother plant. Pod plants, like beans, are ready when the pods are brown and dry. Wind-pollinated plants (such as corn and spinach) and insect-pollinated plants (such as pumpkin and cucumbers) can produce a next generation that looks like a parent, or they can cross-breed with other varieties to get something unique. In recent decades, there has been a significant shift towards the annual purchase of seeds from commercial seed suppliers, and towards hybrid or cloned plants that do not produce seeds that remain "true to the type" - while maintaining the characteristics of the parent- from seeds. Successful seed saving requires the development of new skills, improve the ability of the manufacturer to ensure that the characteristics you want are stored in their system: learning the minimum number of plants to grow to preserve the inherent genetic diversity, recognizing the preferred characteristics of the cultivar grown so that the plants that are not true are not selected for seed production. Recommended minimum number of plants for seed storage: 25 cucumbers, pumpkin, melons; 50-100 radishes, brassicas, mustards; 200 sweet corn. The saved seeds of these plants will reproduce in a true way, provided that the plants were correctly isolated from several varieties of the same species.

Free pollination varieties will become true to type if randomly paired within your own variety. If two varieties of spinach Bloom close to each other, it is likely that the resulting seed is a cross between the two. Several varieties of peppers need to be separated by 500 feet to avoid cross-pollination. The closer the varieties are, the greater the amount of cross seeds. In theory, you should aim at least half a mile between varieties.

Legacy vegetables are varieties grown, selected, saved, named and shared by farmers and gardeners. Legacy plants are now accessible because people have saved seeds for home use in all generations of subsistence farming. You can really reduce your gardening costs by gardening with inheritance seeds that you save from year to year. You can also save seeds of such inherited flowers as: cleome, foxgloves, hollyhock, nasturtium, sweet peas and zinnia. You are in control of the varieties that make the best in your garden. Saving your own seeds increases your self-sufficiency; and you can save money. It is generally accepted that to be an inheritance, a variety must be pollinated in the open air and be at least fifty years old. And since the seeds of inheritance and the practice of saving seeds also have the hope of helping to feed a hungry planet, they are even more convincing today. You can save your favorite hereditary seeds for your use in your garden, increase and improve varieties, exchange with friends, join seed saving organizations or grow seeds commercially at many levels of scale - the possibilities are numerous.

Before storing the seeds, make sure that they have dried thoroughly. Seeds stored at home will retain their vigor if they are thoroughly dried and stored in airtight containers in the freezer for prolonged storage or in a cool, dry cellar for the next season. Although some plant seeds can remain viable for 15 years or more and cereals can remain viable much longer under stable environmental conditions, each year of storage will reduce the amount of seeds that germinate. After processing the seeds and they are ready for packaging for the winter, it is advantageous to purchase dehydrating packs for storage containers in order to keep the seeds dry. seeds should contain 3-5% moisture during storage. The storage of seeds will protect the vegetation of the Earth in the event of global disasters, wars, pandemics and other unforeseen disasters.

Storing seeds can quickly become a hobby, and you will be in good company. Seed saving teaches us the wonder of nature and by saving seeds, we complete the circle of growth. What a wonderful way to end the garden season and look forward to next year's harvests. In addition, storing seeds is a wonderful way to introduce children to gardening.

How to Save Your Garden Seeds

More serious gardeners save seeds. It's easy, it's convenient, and it will save you money. Here are some tips to save money:

Package

Packaged seeds must be stored in their original packaging. Fold the top or use a little adhesive tape to fix the seeds in the package. If the outer carton contains an inner carton, store the leftovers in the outer carton.

Some seeds are much more sensitive to moisture in the air... so, if the seed company took the time to wrap them in bundles of leaves, you should too.

The best place to store packages is in a large saucepan or coffee in the refrigerator. Keep them cool and dry, and most will last for many seasons. Remember that seeds are food, and improper storage will invite all kinds of pests to your basement or pantry.

Home Collection

You can collect and register pollinated cultivars for free; but you can not register the seeds of hybrids. (Well, you can save hybrids, but they won't produce the same hybrid plant they come from... usually you will get one of the mother varieties used to make the hybrid.)

Those collected from free-pollinated varieties of flowers and vegetables can be collected when the fruits or flowers are ripe, or even beyond maturity. They should be relatively dry and free of "litter" as much as possible. You can rinse the seeds of tomato and pepper in a colander and dry them for a day or two on paper napkins or biscuit plates. Those of beans and most flowers do not need special treatment before packing.

Pack in paper envelopes, taking care to label the envelopes to identify the content and year of collection.

Flowers that easily self-sow as annuals, such as celosia plume, are ideal candidates for saving. Just shake the dried flower beds in a large envelope or box, and you will collect hundreds, if not thousands, that can be used in your gardens or shared with friends.

As with packaged seeds, the packaged House should be stored in a cool, dry place and free of insects or rodents. A coffee in the refrigerator is ideal.

Verification of Germination

It is not possible to determine whether a seed will germinate by looking at it. There are two ways for gardeners to control germination. (Germination means that they germinate and grow; the germination percentage is simply the percentage that is vital.)

1. Just put one or two seeds in each cell of a pack of six starter cells and see how many germinate. Or,

2. Place 10-20 seeds between two or more wet paper towels and see how many germinate. The paper towel method is used by virtually all laboratories; however, care must be taken to keep towels wet and warm. You can use a large plastic bag or cellophane to help keep your towels wet.

Check the germination several weeks before the start so you can replace all cultivars that have little or no germination.

Breeding for selection-Ultimate Seed saving

Some people keep the seeds in search of isolating new cultivars. By saving from a flower or fruit that has a specific feature (an almost white marigold or a particularly large pumpkin) you may be able to produce your own crop that reproduces flowers or vegetables with the desired trait. This is the breeding technique known as "selection."The first (almost) white Marigold was produced by a gardener who saved the seeds from the palest yellow marigolds in his gardens for several generations... constantly looking for pale yellow... it was almost white.

How Do Annual, Biennial, and Perennial Plants Differ?

Annual

Let's start with the easiest to grow, annuals, those garden plants that can be grown from seed to maturity, and then let go to sow themselves, during a growing season.

Some plants that are grown as annuals in the garden of middle North America, such as tomatoes, peppers and lima beans, are actually perennials in their native tropics.

Other annuals, such as spinach, lettuce, wheat and some rye plants, can survive a mild winter after autumn sowing and produce seeds in the spring as if they were biennial. Rustic annuals will produce more seeds in mild winter regions when planted in autumn and brought in winter than when ripening in an extremely hot summer climate.

With these exceptions, annuals will bring seeds in the same year they are planted. They do not need special care, only to receive their normal cultural needs and be planted early enough in the season to give them time to ripen the seeds before they are killed by Frost.

Common vegetables that are annual include beans, broccoli, Chinese cabbage, corn, cucumbers, eggplant, lettuce, Muskrat, peas, pepper, pumpkin, most radishes, spinach and pumpkin. Annual flowers include calendula, cosmo, calendula, Spider Flower, sweet pea and zinnia. Growing these annual plants is the best starting point for most gardeners who want to grow seeds.

If you are noticed for a certain crop that does especially well in your garden, try to grow it first for seeds. Peas are a good example or beans. Tomatoes are also a good bet for Seed Savers for the first time, but remember that hybrids should not be grown for seeds. Many gardeners start with sparing only calendula seeds.

To increase your chances of success with vegetables, choose from autogamous annual plants, such as beans, lettuce, peas and tomatoes. The term autogamy means that pollination takes place within each individual and not from other plants. The reason for choosing an autogamous plant is that these plants do not depend on wind or insects to help pollination.

While insects sometimes pollinate some of these autogamous plants, the problem of isolating or separating varieties to avoid crossbreeding is virtually eliminated.

Biennale

Lifting the seed from biennial vegetables requires a little more persistence. These plants bring their edible crop to the season in which they are planted, waiting for the second season to bloom, produce seeds and wither. When the cold in winter is severe, most of the biennial vegetables need to be dug up in the fall and replanted in the spring. Some of them can be left in the garden and covered with a cover of hay or leaves, and they will survive growing the seeds.

In all likelihood, you've probably thought (and grown) of these joint biennials as annuals. They include beets, Brussels sprouts, cabbage, carrots, cauliflower, turnip celery, celery, onion, persil, parsnip, rutabaga, sausage, chard and turnip.

During their second growing season, most biennials bloom in spring and ripen their seeds in full or late summer. The typical biennial flower grows on a sturdy stem that comes from the root or leafy crown of the plant. Stem formation can not be seen, but it is well started in winter after the first growing season of the plant. For a good strong STEM seed plant, the following conditions are usually required:

1. The plant should be a mature and well-developed specimen. Small or immature plants can not form seeds even if they are chilled.

2. A cooling period of at least 30 to 60 days, with temperatures not exceeding 40 ° to 5°. (5 ° to 10 ° C).

3. Moderate climate prevailing during the period of new spring growth of the mother plant.

Biennials are a new complication for the seed producer. It is necessary to bring the vegetable during the winter in good condition so that it blooms and yields seeds the next year.

This can be as simple as growing salesforce, so sturdy that a cover of hay or leaves will protect the roots in the garden during the worst northern winters. Or it can be as difficult as growing cauliflower, which in the North will not survive outdoors and which can not be stored in a root cellar.

Cauliflower should be grown for an outdoor season, then transplanted into a cold frame or greenhouse for the winter, and then planted again outdoors in the spring.

Perennials

Perennials return year after year, growing from underground parts that live during the winter. Most perennials planted from seeds will begin to produce seeds themselves a year or two after planting. Rhubarb and asparagus are the most frequently cultivated perennial garden vegetables. There are dozens of perennial herbaceous flowers such as daylily, iris, delphinium and peony. New varieties are developed by professional and amateur plant breeders using seeds. These improved varieties are then preserved as true clones of the mother plant using vegetative propagation methods such as division or cuttings. The description of vegetative propagation techniques goes beyond the scope of this book; an excellent source for this information are the secrets of plant propagation by Lewis Hill (Garden Way Publishing, 1985).

Seed Saving Technical

Once you've decided which crops and varieties you want to save the seeds from, Make seeds save part of your garden plan. It's easy to do and you will get the best results if you plan ahead. Understand how you may need to adjust the timing of planting, collect the necessary equipment for harvesting and cleaning the seeds, and decide where and how to store the seeds.

Think in terms of five steps:

Phase 1. Take care of your plants so that they produce high-quality seeds.

Phase 2. Collect the seeds.

Phase 3. Clean the seeds and let them dry.

Phase 4. Pack and store seeds.

Phase 5. Test the vitality of the seeds and get ready to plant!

The details of each step vary from the harvest, and this is a fun part, but first, let's look at each stage of the process in detail.

Growing Large Seeds

Reward the crops you grow for the first seed spot on your gardening priority list for the season. Seed plants above all deserve good care because they are the model for successful gardening in the future.

Think of a time when you paid a bargain price for a package of six plants that were beyond their first. Chances are the case turned out to be a nuisance. Even with greater care and attention, these sunken and weak plants probably did not bounce very well and the harvest was a disappointment. The same applies to seeds: if you start with weak seeds, your harvest will be disadvantaged from the very beginning. On the contrary, the stronger the seed you grow, the better your future harvest will be.

For many types of vegetables, the care you give to cultivated plants for the production of seeds is no different from what you give to cultivated plants for a regular harvest. Provide good soil, avoid water stress and take measures to avoid pest problems (such as using row cover or applying compost tea), and you get good results.

Some crops, however, need special treatment to be the best seed producers. You may need to plant them in a different season than usual, or you may need to control the pollination process.

Some crops have tall, heavy seed stems that need support. And most biennial crops need protection to survive wintering.

Label every step of the way

It is a smart idea to get into the habit of using plant labels and keep records throughout the gardening season. When you look at the plants in your garden, you may find it easy to tell which variety of tomato is that even without checking a label, but it is almost impossible to distinguish the seeds of one variety from another only in appearance. You may also have difficulty identifying which culture is that. Seeds of cabbage and broccoli are very similar, for example, just like many types of pumpkin seeds. It is much more fun to share seeds with others when you can identify seeds with confidence and a correct ID is essential if you want to record particular varieties of inheritance.

Stock up on plant labels early in the season and keep a stock in your seed starting area and gardening tote. Label seedlings in pots, rows and beds in the garden. Also put a colored thread or warning tape in your garden tote. As the season progresses, use wire or tape to mark the individual plants from which you want to save the seed.

When harvesting, write the name of the crop and Variety on the labels and place it on the buckets, bags and other containers in which you collect the seed heads. Label the scattered seeds for drying on plates or sieves. And as a final step, label the packages of seeds ready for storage.

Selection of Seed Parents

Seed selection is at the heart of any program Seed Garden. If you are careful in choosing the seed you save from your garden, you can not only perpetuate and multiply your garden plants, but also improve and perfect them. Of course, you will want to save the seed of your best plants, because higher plants are more likely to produce seeds that will develop into another generation of plants with the same desirable characteristics.

If you plan to save seeds from the garden, do not wait for autumn to select mother plants. Monitor the plants throughout the growing season, keeping in mind the qualities that you want to encourage the most. To select the best plants, you need to know how they performed throughout the season.

Consider the whole plant

This is the whole plant, rather than a single isolated fruit, which you should consider when selecting. For example, when choosing a tomato plant, you want to save the seed from a vine that bore a lot of excellent fruits, not just from a single huge fruit that drew your attention to the edge of the plot.

The succulent and early plant that you would choose before eating is the one from which you should save the seed. This is not always easy to do, especially when the family loudly asks for the first Sweet Corn. Many gardeners who regularly save the seed see enough of an improvement in plants grown from the seed that they choose to make the sacrifice useful. If you are not particularly ready to grow an early strain, however, preferring to select only for flavor or other quality, or if the species is self-pollinating like tomato, then of course, you can go ahead and feast on these first fruits from your garden.

If you save root seeds-carrot, beet, turnip, rutabaga, celery turnip, parsnip, salsify-biennial, you will have to dig and store the roots during the winter, unless you live in an area where winters are mild. Select the roots for the desirable qualities that you store, and then select them again from the roots preserved in the spring, choosing for your first seed those that remained in good shape during the entire storage period. People who save potatoes for planting will make the same choices.

You will have the best chances of with cabbages and other cruciferous trees if you let them grow to eat, or almost, before crossing the winter in your garden or in the cold cellar. Vegetable plants that overwinter above in an immature state do not always bloom and reliably put the seed next spring. Biennial flowers for the collection of seeds remain in the garden throughout their life cycle.

More than One

If you are going to save the seed from your garden each year, experts advise that it would be wise to keep the seeds of more than one plant of the same variety, even if you only need a few seeds, in order to keep a genetic basis for the most extensive your experiments to improve the garden. This is especially true for corn.

There are two exceptions to this rule. Autogamous plants such as beans and peas are inbred by nature, and therefore all seeds could be saved by a plant without fear of spoilage. If healthy and productive plants are chosen, the seeds should improve the quality. The checklist on page 137 lists common seed-borne diseases to be controlled. Rogue out (remove) all diseased seed plants. The second exception is with pumpkins and pumpkins. Seeds of a pumpkin or pumpkin can be saved without any changes in the quality of plants the following year.

What About Hybrids?

Domestic gardeners are usually advised not to save seeds from hybrid crops. The offspring of hybrid plants, especially corn, is sometimes sterile. When transporting fertile seeds, this seed will produce plants unlike the mother plant. The product of a cross between hybrid plants often comes to resemble one of its ancestors.

Since the reason for the growth of hybrid seeds is usually the exceptional vigor found in the first generation after crossing, there would be little to gain from the reproduction of hybrids towards their parents and grandparents.

There's certainly no harm in saving the hybrid seed, though. If you like to experiment, go ahead and plant these seeds. Don't expect big things from this second generation, but keep your eyes open and you could grow something you want. You should not depend on the saved seed of a hybrid crop, however, if you want to be sure to harvest what you need next year.

Records of the type and number of plants from which the seed is harvested, as well as any other relevant data, such as yield or early-onset assessments of parent plants, should be kept at the time of seed registration. This will help you evaluate the results of your seed saving efforts after following the practice for a few years.

Factory Quality

There are many good qualities to look for when selecting plants from which to save the seed. It is recommended to take into account at least some of the following characteristics when choosing mother plants:

1. Flavor

2. Performance

3. Go ahead

4. Color

5. Size

6. Service of life

7. Resistance to disease

8. Insect resistance

9. Early bearing (fruits, heads, flowers, etc.)

10. Late in bolting seeds (lettuce, etc.)

11. Good germination in bad weather

12. Absence of plugs, plugs, etc.

13. Seeds-few and small in juicy fruits, large for sunflowers

14. Consistency, tenderness, juiciness

15. Employability. For example, a tomato and should be dry and fleshy. Flint corn should dry well. Cursed Kraut would be solid. The flowers to be cut must remain erect.

16. Stature-tall, dwarf, intermediate

17. Weather tolerance, drought position

18. Aromatic appeal

Saving Seeds from Your Garden

For many gardeners, the garden begins in January when the first seed catalog arrives in the mailbox. As the cold wind howls outside, we retreat to a comfortable chair and browse the catalog, carefully observing the varieties of lettuce and tomatoes to try to wish that we had the space to plant each flower so skillfully displayed on its pages.

But have you ever wondered where your great-grandparents acquired seeds for their gardens, before there were catalogs of seeds and fancy gardening centers?

They saved the seeds for the next year from their own garden!

Saving seeds from your own flowers or vegetables is a wonderful way to fully live the growth cycle of plants. It is also much cheaper than buying seeds every spring, and the seeds of your plants will be well adapted to the peculiarities of the growing conditions of your garden. Not only that, it is also a fairly simple process.

Keep seeds only from vigorous and healthy plants. Some plant diseases can be repaired in the seeds where they will then be passed on to the next generation of plants. So do not save the seeds of a plant that is obviously sick or has struggled all season. Choose the seeds of plants that have the characteristics you want, such as height, robustness, early or late ripening, flavor or vigor.

It is not recommended to store seeds of hybrid plants. Hybrids are the result of crossing two genetically different mother plants, both severely inbred to concentrate desirable characteristics. The first generation, called hybrid F1, is superior to parents. But subsequent generations of plants grown from saved seeds of an F1 plant tend to casually return to the characteristics of the original ancestor plants.

Plants that are not Hybrid are called free pollination. Many seed catalogs will identify which of their seeds are hybrid or pollinated in the open air. If you are going to save your seed, always start with open pollinated seeds. Some of them can be identified as seed inheritance. These inherited varieties have been handed down for generations, often saved within the same family for many years before becoming accessible to the general public.

Cross-pollination is another concern for the gardener who saves seeds. Cross-pollination often gives seeds that have a different genetic composition than the mother plant. Pumpkins, pumpkins and small pumpkins can cross each other, which gives seeds that will grow to produce rather picturesque fruits. Sweet corn intersects with field corn or popcorn, and your 6-inch marigolds intersect with your neighbor's 18-inch pompom marigolds. However, the crossing will only take place within one species. Cucumbers do not intersect with pumpkin, and the cosmos does not intersect with thoughts.

To avoid cross-pollination, keep two varieties of the same species separated by as much space as possible. Some species, such as corn, are wind-pollinated and pollen can travel great distances. These plants must be pollinated by hand and isolated from other varieties of their species. This can be done with corn, for example, by attaching a small paper bag to the selected ears before the Silk emerges, and then once the Silk has appeared, it is hand-pollinated with pollen of the same plant or its healthy neighbors.

Seeds should be collected on a dry, sunny day. Frost does not hurt most seeds until the seed remains dry. Vegetables such as cucumbers, peppers and tomatoes should become slightly overripe before their seeds are harvested. Flower seeds and vegetable seeds such as lettuce should be collected after the seed heads have become dry, but do not wait too long, as many will break, which means that they will be dropped from the seed or seed if they stay on the plant for too long.

Seeds of cucumber, pumpkin, tomato need one more step before they are ready for storage. First, the seeds must be separated from the pulp, and then dried. Collect the seeds of these vegetables, pulp and everything. Put the mess in a container with water and mix well, then let it stand a little. The pulp will rise upwards while the seeds will flow downwards. Carefully pour the pulp and repeat the process until most of the pulp has been poured. Then drain the seeds and put them on the newspapers to dry.

Seeds should be kept as dry as possible. Give all the seeds after the harvest drying period of at least a week, just to be sure that they are dry. Spread them on a plate of paper or newspapers in a warm place away from the sun while drying.

It is very important to keep the seed dry during storage. Store dry seeds in tightly closed jars, metal film containers or old vitamin bottles. To save space, small amounts of different varieties of seeds can be stored in separate bags inside a jar. A cool, but never frozen garage, a closed spare room or a cool basement can all be good places to store seeds. Or just keep the sealed seed jars in the refrigerator. Temperatures between 32 and 41 degrees Fahrenheit are ideal.

Be sure to label the pots and envelopes so that when spring comes back, you know what seeds of flowers and vegetables you plant, and include the date when the seeds were collected. Some seeds remain viable for several years, but most will pass better if planted immediately next spring.

Try to save the vegetable seeds or flowers from your garden this year and make them grow next season. This infinite cycle can allow you to realize the infinite joy of gardening through all seasons and all stages of a plant's life.

Saving Seeds From Your Herb Garden

Many gardeners like to save the seeds they collected in their herb gardens. This way they have many seeds to plant next year. When the seeds are fully ripe and fragrant, it's time to collect the seeds. Looking for mature seeds for harvesting is an enjoyable experience, and you'll have plenty of seeds to cut and save for planting during the next gardening season.

When the flowers of the plant are almost completely ripe, cut the stems of the plants at the base. Tie the ends of the rods with a strong elastic band or rope. Cover the flower beds with a paper bag attached to the plant with a rope or rope, then hang the package upside down in a dry, dark place like an attic.

In a couple of weeks, take the package of plants with covered flower buds. Shake the package well to free the seeds from the flower buds. The seeds will be turned towards the bottom of the attached brown paper bag. You will be able to use the saved seeds for the next gardening season if you store them in paper packages or envelopes in an airtight container. Place the airtight container in a dark place, until the seeds are used. Be sure to label each package or envelope with the type of seeds you registered and the date you stored them to facilitate planting in the next year.

Some plants do not easily move away from seeds. It is therefore important to know if the plants you want in your garden easily start from the seeds. Ask your local nursery if the grass you want to grow starts easily from the seeds. Otherwise, you will have to buy seedlings. Some of the herbs that easily move away from the seeds are lavender, basil, coriander and chives.

Plants grow better from self-pollinating seeds. Since many herbs pollinate, you should be able to collect a large selection of seeds from your garden. But do not collect seeds of plants pollinated by bees. Cross-pollination that occurs from bee pollination can give you unwanted surprises when your plants grow and grow.

If you have had seeds for a year or two, you may want to check if they are still viable for planting. Take the seeds and put them in a wet paper towel inside a perforated plastic bag. If they germinate in a few days, the seeds are still good and will produce plants. If they do not, discard the seeds. If only some of the seeds produce shoots, you may need to plant more seeds than usual to get the number of plants you want.

Do not save seeds of hybrid plants. Seeds of hybrid plants do not reproduce the same plant as the mother plant. But if you have healthy or rare plants in your garden that you want to breed, saving seeds is a great way to get more plants without buying seeds. Saving from seeds is the only way to get rare or old plant varieties that can not be found even in nurseries.

Save Seeds - How to Preserve Seeds for Tomatoes

Saving tomato seeds for the next season is a simple task. It can be made for the vegetable garden and for your commercial harvest. If you want to save the seeds and get better results; you need to follow a few simple, but important rules. Here are some useful information that will help you develop a healthy tomato culture for the coming seasons.

To get seeds; we need to know how to extract them from tomatoes. This is a long but simple procedure that can be easily practiced at home. Try to find those tomatoes that come from the healthiest plants; for they will be the strongest contenders to reproduce a healthy harvest for the next season. Let the larger ones ripen until their skin becomes wrinkled, then pick them up. Do not choose tomatoes that have fallen because they would not give good seeds.

Now extract the seeds from the selected tomatoes. Gently cut and extract the seeds of tomatoes with pulp and gel around them. Now put them in a glass and cover with a paper plate or cheese cloth, in order to avoid dust and leave it for two or three days.

Fill the glass with water and let the seeds separate from the pulp, then filter the seeds by draining the water. Gently clean them and spread the seeds on a flat, dry surface. Let them dry for about a week. After about seven days, do their drought test, choose a seed and fold it. If it bends, it is still wet. In case of breakage, it is dry and ready for storage, or give it another day to dry. The weather will be dictated by the temperature and humidity levels in your area.

Now it's time to store the seeds. It is necessary to have clean and airtight containers or envelopes to save seeds. Take a clean and dry container. make sure that there is no more moisture after cleaning the container because if it remains a little dirty or wet; the seed will not remain more useful due to mold or fungus. After putting them in the container, label with the name of the tomato variety and do not forget to mention the duration of storage. Now, when the seeds are well stored, choose a safe place for the container that must be a dark and cold place, as moisture and Heat are the enemies of the seeds. You can put them in your refrigerator, your seeds, the will remain until the next season.

Save Tomato Seeds

It's no secret that I like to save the seeds and prefer to grow varieties of vegetables for taste, rather than a strong resistance to yield or resistance to disease.

Here's how to do it (don't forget to label everything):

Place tomato seeds in a glass mason or other medium-large jar (it is acceptable to include tomato mud).

Fill the pot with 2/3 plenty of water.

Leave to rest at room temperature to ferment for a few days for up to a week. It will probably smell bad as it ferments, so place it accordingly. The fermentation process will eliminate the viscous coating of the seeds, which is crucial to preserve them successfully so that they germinate next spring.

After about a week, the vital seeds will sink to the bottom and the unwanted tomato pulp will fluctuate.

Carefully fill the pot with water (in the sink) so that the moldy things on top overflow from the pot.

Strain the seeds on trial and rinse the seeds thoroughly.

Put the seeds outstretched and rinse on a plate and spread them out to dry. This can take from a few days to a week. Again, this is crucial to successfully conserve the seeds until next spring.

Once dry, wrap the seeds in labeled envelopes. Avoid storing in plastic bags to reduce the risk of mold.

Store seeds in a cool, dry place.

One final note on tomato savings: make sure the seeds you save come from the variety of cultural goods. Hybrid tomato seeds (labeled F1 on seed packaging) do not produce plants such as seeds.

Start tomato seeds 8 to 10 weeks before the average date of your last spring frost. Transplant every three weeks into the next size dish. They will double in size each week and should be about 12 to 18 inches tall when it is time for them to be transplanted outdoors.

The first ones I have ever harvested seeds from. Since then, they have been planted and reassembled several times. This is the best part of growing heritage vegetables: you just have to buy the seeds once.

Seed Harvest

One that you have selected the plants from which you intend to save the seeds, the first step is to identify the chosen plants so that they do not accidentally end up in the soup pot or the composition of the flowers before you have had the opportunity to collect the seed you want. Some gardeners attach a cloth or light wire to their individuals who produce elite seeds. Others mark the plant with a pole. Make sure the rest of your family knows which plants should not be harvested.

Time

Your next concern will be to determine the right time to harvest the seeds. Seeds harvested too early, before they have time to ripen, will not have had the opportunity to accumulate enough stored food to start well, or even to last the entire winter. These seeds are likely to be thin and light in weight. It will be less likely to survive storage, germinate well or produce solid seedlings.

So you want your seed to be well ripened before picking it up, but not so far away that it falls to the ground or blows from the wind.

In general, seed garden plants will fall into one of three groups, depending on how they ripen their fruit:

Plants with seeds incorporated into fleshy fruits, such as tomatoes, eggs and peppers. These soft fruits should be left to turn quite ripe, even a little too ripe, before the seeds are harvested. Fruits should be slightly soft, but should not be so ripe that they begin to warm up. It is also important not to let the fruit dry around the seed, or it can form a hard cover that will affect the shelf life of the seed.

Seed crops, such as corn, wheat, beans and others where the seed is the edible part of the plant. These plants usually hold their seeds for a while after reaching maturity, giving you the chance to make your collection more or less when you choose, until the seed has become completely dry. Mature plants with dry seeds that tend to rely on wind or rain can be cut and stacked in heal and dry further before removing the seed.

Plants that break easily, despairing of mature seeds as soon as they reach maturity. Lettuce, onions, okra and members of the mustard family, as well as many flowers, not only lay their ripe seeds quickly as soon as they are dry; they also tend to gradually ripen the seeds so that a single plant will usually have a good pair of hanging bitter seeds as the ripe seeds fall out.

To be sure to catch a good crop of seeds from these plants, you need to inspect them every day and collect ripe seeds in small amounts in a paper bag as it prepares, or attach a broken paper bag to the seed head. The seeds they collect in the bag may still contain immature specimens, but these can usually be scanned by pouring the seed from one container to another in a breeze. Some plants in this group, especially those in the Mustard family, will need a pole to support the seed stem. When harvesting most seeds, try to do the work on a dry and sunny day after the dew has evaporated. However, the seeds of the plants in the group three above are often harvested when they are wet to avoid seed loss. Although most of the seeds you harvest in the fall will not be affected by the low temperature of a slight frost, the frost can cause a build-up of moisture that will reduce the quality of the seeds.

To avoid confusion, label each batch of seeds as soon as possible after harvest, especially if you save more than one variety of a species, such as different varieties of tomatoes or peppers or different members of the mustard family, whose seeds are very similar.

Seed Extraction and Drying

Your first job, after harvesting fruits containing seeds such as tomatoes, peppers, pumpkin and melons, is to separate the seed from the pulp. Scrape off the lean part of the fruit and save the rest of the overripe meat for your hens or put it on the compost heap. It's a good idea to let tomato seeds and pulp ferment for three or four days, to help control bacterial cancer. To do this, pour the lean tomato pulp into a saucepan, add about ¼ cup of water and observe, in the next few days, that the light pulp and unnecessary seeds rise and flow heavier and good seeds.

Some gardeners also allow cucumber and melon seeds to ferment, using the same procedure. You can also fork, seeds and wash them.

For pumpkin and pumpkins, separate the seeds from the pulp, wash them thoroughly to remove any traces of plant material and dry them. large seeds should dry for five to six days. The smallest can be ready in three to four days.

Peas, beans, soybeans and lime are usually removed from the dried pods by threshing. Don't be too rough on these seeds, though. Internal injuries of seeds are more likely with machine treatment, but can occur when force is used to remove seeds from their envelopes. Damage to the seed may not be noticeable, but if the stem or embryonic root is bruised, the seed may germinate poorly or produce rickets seedlings.

Seeds of lettuce, sunflower, dill, calendula and other dry-harvested plants can be shaken through a cloth screen to sift the sequins.

Removal of unwanted light seeds and parts of the STEM and leaves, as well as pulp, can be carried out by floating. When you put the seeds in the water, the glitter, the "loss" of seeds and pulp increases, and the right seeds flow. Seeds other than tomatoes that you treat in this way should be quickly distributed for drying.

Moisture

As already mentioned, excess moisture in the seed will reduce its quality. Seed it is not dry enough so stored will keep poorly and have a low percentage of germination. A moisture content of more than 20% will cause heat from the seeds stored in bulk. Most seeds do better if they are stored with a moisture content of 8-15%. It is important to dry all the seeds that you will keep well-even already dried seeds such as dill and carrot.

You will not be able to tell the exact moisture content of the seed in house conditions, of course, but you can give your seeds a long period of complete drying before storage, and this should be enough. The important thing to remember is not to pack any harvested seed until it has had at least a few days of Air drying after being removed from the plant. The larger the seed, the longer the drying period.

Most seeds, in most climates, dry properly for storage at home if they spread on paper towels or newspapers in a ventilated place for a week. They need to be turned over and possibly spread on dry fresh paper (depending on the type of seed) several times during this period.

If you have been forced to pick up your seeds in rainy weather or if you live in a humid climate, you can use mild heat to dry some of your seeds such as corn and other cereals. However, this heat should be adjusted so that it never exceeds 100 ° F. (38 ° C) , and 90 ° F. (32 ° C.) is preferable. Too fast drying can cause shrinkage and rupture of the seed and the formation of a hard, impermeable and undesirable integument. Drying at too high temperatures will negatively affect the vitality and vigor of the seed.

A much safer method of accelerating the drying process is to spread the seed in the sun, on screens or on a flat roof or on the sidewalk, for a day or two of intensive drying.

Many Seed Savers use silica gel (available in many pharmacies or grocery stores, crafts or hardware stores) as a desiccant. Mix the air-dried seeds in an airtight container with an equal weight of silica gel. Most of the silica gel is processed to transform the color when it has absorbed its maximum moisture. Silica Gel can be oven dried to be reused.

After the seeds have dried, do not let them sit in the fresh air, otherwise they will absorb moisture from the room.

Storage of Seeds

Now that you have grown, selected, harvested and dried your seeds, it's time to store them. Poorly dried seeds can deteriorate significantly during the winter. If you rely on homemade seeds for your spring plantations or try to perform an inherited strain of a particular vegetable, the loss of a year's seed crop can be disastrous.

Seeds, remember, continue their basic vital processes even in dormancy, but at a very low rate. The moisture they absorb from the air combines with the Stored food to form a soluble food, which then combines with oxygen from the air to release carbon dioxide, water and heat.

Since your seeds exchange elements and gases with the atmosphere while they are dormant, your goal in conserving them should be to limit these exchanges to the minimum necessary to maintain life in the seed. This means avoiding any stimulation that would encourage the seed to accelerate its metabolism, or that would damage the embryo. If the stored seeds need to be protected from moisture and heat, as well as from insects and other animals that would like to eat them.

Humidity

Let's consider moisture first. As mentioned above, the presence of moisture triggers the formation of soluble compounds in the plant. Too much moisture in the air will cause the seed to burn its stored food at too fast a speed, producing excess heat which further reduces the seed's ability to germinate.

How much moisture is too much? Seeds differ, depending on their variety, in their ability to absorb water from the air, even under the same conditions of temperature and humidity. Beans, peas and cereals (including corn) should not contain more than 13% moisture for safe storage. Soy should have a little less-12.5 percent - and peanuts and most other vegetables even less moisture - about 9 percent, with 4-6% be considered ideal for long-term storage.

According to Dr. James Harrington, a seed expert, every 1% reduction in Seed Moisture, less than 14% but not less than 5%, doubles the lifespanhope for most vegetable seeds. Lowering the moisture content below 1 or 2% adversely affects the viability of the seed. Seeds are unlikely to dry out unless artificial heat is applied. Even if gardeners have no way to accurately determine the moisture content of a seed, we can use these figures as a guide.

Once the seed has been dried for storage, it must be kept as dry as possible. If the seeds can get wet after the initial drying, they will lose part of their longevity, even if they are dried again. Sealed and moisture-resistant containers, such as cans and jars, are the best place to store seeds, but only if the seeds are good and dry before being set aside. Wet seeds, stored in covered containers, deteriorate faster than dry seeds in open storage.

Silica gel can be used in the permanent storage container-equal parts by weight of seeds and silica. Many gardeners put the seeds in well-marked paper bags and store them in tight containers with loose silica gel on the bottom.

Temperature

The storage temperature also affects the quality of storage of seeds. Most seeds can tolerate cold conditions and even frosts that would kill the mother plant, sometimes from 0 ° F. (-18 ° C), as long as they are completely dry. Excess moisture in a seed subjected to freezing temperatures can freeze and damage the seed.

Dr. Harrington has found that at a relative humidity of 70% or less, it is possible to double the life of the seed for every 9 ° F. (5 ° C.) decrease in temperature in the range of 32 ° to 112 ° F. (0 ° to 44.5 ° C.)

It follows, therefore, that heat especially when combined with high humidity the is the enemy of seed quality. The high temperatures not only accelerate the internal chemistry of the seed; they also promote the activity of fungi, bacteria and insects that further compromise the vitality of the seed by adding the heat of their breaths, and sometimes by excreting chemicals or other by-products that harm the embryo or soften the tegument.

Fungi grow in 13-16 percent humidity at temperatures from 85 ° to 95 ° F. (30 ° to 35 ° C.) slow down to 70 ° F. (21 ° C.) and barely exist at 50 ° F (10 ° C.) different bacteria grow at different temperatures, but all of them need a high content of bacteria.

Long-term storage in the refrigerator or freezer is the best solution, until the moisture content of the seed is low, and the container you use is vapor-tight. When removing the seeds from the freezer, leave the container closed while the seeds heat up to room temperature, otherwise condensation will form on the seeds.

Insect

Invasive insects can be prevented by storing seeds in tightly closed containers. If the eggs of insects are already present in the seeds, they can be discouraged by maintaining a temperature not exceeding 40 ° to 5 ° F. (from 5 ° to 10 ° C.), at what level most insects that could affect the seed would be relatively inactive. Freezing, of course, destroys or completely immobilizes insects.

From the previous sections, you can see that the vitality of a seed, far from being an absolute value, strongly depends on the storage conditions — not only in the first year, but for the life of the seed. For example, onion seeds, generally considered short-lived, were stored for up to 12 years when they are dry and well sealed, but deteriorate within a few months when stored at high temperatures in a damp place.

Points to remember

To get the best results with your preserved garden seeds, we recommend doing the following:

1. Store dry seeds well.

2. Do not allow the seeds to moisten after initial drying.

3. Keep the storage temperature as low as possible.

4. Keep the storage area as dry as possible, especially if the temperature is below the freezing point.

5. Label all containers with Variety, date and any other registered strain.

6. If you keep the seeds in envelopes, store the entire collection in a well-covered can of lard, a large jar of mayonnaise (often available in restaurants) or another sealed container.

7. Peas and beans are best stored in bags rather than in airtight containers.

8.If you keep the seeds for more than a year, be sure to protect morepossible heat and humidity during the summer.

From these guidelines, you can see that a great place to store seeds is your refrigerator or freezer.

Also, the refrigerator is a great place to store commercial seeds left by summer gardening activities. Put the bags of seeds in a box and cover them.

Dried Seed Collection

Dry seeds are simple to collect as long as you know that the seeds can break, break and release their seeds. Just choose large seeds like pea pods and collect them in a container. For small seeds introduced into the seed heads, such as carrots and lettuce, you can collect individual seeds if only a small amount is needed. If you want to save large quantities, try cutting whole stems (a pair of hand pruners works well for cutting stiff stems) and bringing them inside for complete drying. To minimize the risk of seed loss when cutting the stems, dip the stems upside down in a bucket or paper bag while cutting them. It is better to cut the plants rather than extract them from the roots, because the soil that has clung to the roots can eventually mix with the seed, and it is better to avoid it (See page 38 for why).

Collection of Wet Seeds

"Wet" seeds are enclosed in a fruit. For some wet seed crops, seed cultivation is the same as the cultivation of ripe fruit for consumption. For other crops, such as cucumbers, the seeds are not ready to be harvested simultaneously with the fruits. The fruits you eat contain immature seeds. When the fruit is completely ripe from a physiological point of view and the seeds are ripe, you would not want to eat this fruit. It would taste sour and could start to ferment inside.

Seed Cleaning and Drying

Cleaning and drying seeds are fun projects, and it's a good thing, because seeds that are not dry and clean may not store well. The techniques used to clean dry seeds are different from those used to clean wet seeds.

Cleaning Dry Seeds

"Dirty seed" is a seed mixed with pieces of Pula from the head of the flower and pieces of STEM and leaf. It is not essential that you know-evaluate the seeds of Pula, but there are good reasons why it is worth it:

* Pula may be moist or tend to absorb moisture more easily than seeds alone.

* Pula may have disease spores or mold clinging to it.

* Pula may clog a seeder.

* Pula throws away the weight of the seed (this is more important for commercial producers than for producers).

Two ways to separate seeds and sequins are by weight, with a process called threading and pruning, using screens.

Seeds can also end up mixed with the soil, but it is better to prevent this from happening in the first place, if possible.

Like tallow, the soil can contain moisture and carry diseases. But the soil tends to be heavy, so it is not easy to separate the soil from the seeds by tapping.

Separation of the Slope

A fun way to separate seeds from tallow is to roll the seed on a slope. It works best with round seeds, such as radishes, broccoli and arugula. All you need is a shallow pan or bowl and a newspaper section or kitchen chopping board or other smooth board.

Vannage

If you stand out on a windy day with a stone in one hand and a leaf in the other and let them go, what pens? The stone will fall directly to your feet, and the Leaf will move away from it and gradually fall to the ground. This is the principle behind vannage.

Some types of seeds are much heavier than the tallow surrounding them. In such cases, you can separate the seeds from the sequins by pouring them through a slight airflow. The seeds will fall to the ground closer to you while the tallow will travel a little further. You can try to work with a natural breeze, but using a small electric fan gives you more control.

How to Separate By Slope

1. Pour a few seeds and sequins on one end of a newspaper sheet or a board.

2. Take the newspaper or table and gently tilt the other end over the pan or bowl.

3. Increase the slope, so that the seeds begin to roll on the slope. They should accelerate and reach the container before the ball. With a little practice, you'll probably find it easy to hone your technique.

Like Winnow

1.Install the vannage Station: Place a small electric fan on a table, lay a sheet or tarpaulin on the floor next to the table and place two important containers on the tarpaulin side by side. An outdoor terrace is a great place because you can simply leave excess straw.

2.Put the seeds and sequins in a bowl, bucket or small basket.

3.Set the fan to a minimum and gently pour the seeds and straw in front of the air flow.

4.Do not pour too much material on the first attempt. Stop and check the results. The goal is to make the best use of the seed in the container closest to the fan and bring the balloon into the second container. Inevitably, some even drink from Wild shot which is why the carpet is a good idea.

If most of the straw is in the first container with seeds, the draft was too soft. Put all this container in your pouring container, mount the fan one step and try again.

5.Repeat the tests until you are satisfied with the results.

Kind reader,

Thank you very much. I hope you enjoyed the book.

Can I ask you a big favor?

I would be grateful if you would please take a few minutes to leave me a gold star on Amazon.

Thank you again for your support.

Andrew McDeere

Made in the USA
Coppell, TX
25 January 2022